UNDERSTAND HOW TO DRAW DS9

Drawing
Landscapes

Ray Campbell Smith

SEARCH PRESS

Introduction

The urge to create distinguishes man from the beasts and from the dawn of history homo sapiens has sought to express himself in art. Cave drawings – some of them wonderfully preserved for thousands of years – bear eloquent and vivid witness to this instinct for art that is in all of us. Almost from the cradle, children will draw and some of their untutored images are inventive and original. As other interests and responsibilities begin to crowd in, this creative urge may fade, sometimes assisted by unimaginative teaching, as boring sessions spent drawing the staffroom teapot begin to take their toll! But the instinct is still there, if dormant, and growing numbers of people, both young and old, are constantly discovering the joy and satisfaction of artistic creation. Many more long to try their hand but are deterred by lack of confidence and by the often mistaken conviction that they lack the necessary talent. In this little book I hope to convince them that artistic skill can be successfully developed, often from unpromising beginnings.

The basis of all good art is sound draughtsmanship and the development of skill with the pencil is the proper starting point. For those to whom paints and brushes are a mystery, it makes good sense to begin with the simpler tools required for line drawing and it cannot be too strongly emphasized that continuous practice is the only sure road to progress. So whenever you can, take a sketch book with you on your travels and record quick line impressions of any and every subject that appeals to you. Your standard will improve with this regular practice and some of the sketches may well be of subsequent use for incorporating into more ambitious projects. Always remember that we are less concerned with exactness and mechanical accuracy than we are with feeling, so give full rein to your imagination and to your response to that aspect of your subject that first appealed to you. If this results in a little exaggeration, so be it, for if we cannot convey our emotional reaction in our drawing, we will not elicit much response from others. The image that first excited us may be a mass of sunlit foliage against the sombre grey of a cloud-shadowed hill; a pattern of fields of varying textures and colours, or any one of a thousand other interesting shapes or dramatic contrasts. Whatever it may be, it must be strongly emphasized so that our drawing proclaims, *"This* is what captured my imagination".

Cave paintings

Beechwood

Drawing materials

The beginner instinctively thinks of the graphite pencil as the normal tool for drawing and undoubtedly it is the most widely used, but there is a wide variety of other drawing implements on the market. All have advantages and some disadvantages and it is a good plan to try out as many as you can. Some will suit your style better than others and some will be more suitable for particular subjects.

Pencils: these are made in many grades according to their hardness or softness. The hardest pencil, the lightest, is a 6H and the softest, or darkest, a 7B. Hard pencils are used for very fine, exact work, such as machine and architectural drawings. For sketching purposes I normally use an HB, (if some detail is required), a 2B and either a 4B or a 6B.

Then there are the carbon pencils and the Conté pencils, which also come in several grades and these are useful for depicting deep shadows. Conté pencils are made in sepia and white as well as black.

Crayons: these are manufactured in both pencil and stick form, in a full range of colours. Watercolour crayons are water-soluble and the black is a particularly useful drawing tool, for the marks it makes can be softened and modified by the application of a wet brush – a technique that can produce interesting and attractive effects.

Charcoal: this is an extremely useful drawing implement for conveying broad impressions quickly and dramatically. However, it has the disadvantage of smudging all too easily – a quality shared by pastels and, to a lesser extent, by soft pencils and by carbon and Conté pencils. The problem can be partly overcome by the use of an aerosol spray fixative. Incidentally, an ordinary hair spray will do the job quite satisfactorily and rather more cheaply.

Pens: the nibs vary greatly, both in shape and in their degree of flexibility. You should avoid those that produce a rather mechanical line of uniform thickness, such as ballpoint pens and some fountain pens. A soft, flexible nib which can produce both fine and heavy lines, according to the amount of pressure exerted, is infinitely preferable and far more expressive.

Inks: these come in a variety of colours, some waterproof when dry, some water-soluble. Waterproof inks are normally used for line and wash work, so that the drawing is not disturbed by the addition of subsequent washes. Black ink is the most commonly used but sepia and other browns are useful for softer effects.

I often use a stick of balsa wood, sharpened to a point, as a drawing implement. Dipped in Indian ink and used on a rough paper it produces a pleasantly broken line, and as the ink on the stick begins to run out, a softer line, akin to charcoal, results. This greyish line is useful for rendering lighter passages, such as clouds, distant hills and the like.

Brushes: some types may be used as drawing implements and can produce flexible and often beautiful lines. They can also be used for adding tonal washes to black and white drawings.

Papers: these are manufactured in a wide variety of weights and surfaces and with experience and experiment you will discover those that suit you best. I find watercolour paper with what is termed a 'Not', (cold press), finish most sympathetic, for the slight roughness of its surface produces a rather grainy line: a smooth, (hot press), paper usually gives rise to a harder, more uncompromising line.

If you intend to use water – for modifying the marks made by a water-soluble implement, or for adding tonal washes – remember to use a heavier weight of paper, to avoid the problem of cockling.

Rubbers: these are frowned upon by many teachers and should be used as little as possible. But we all need them sometimes and then it is as well to have one that will damage the surface of the paper as little as possible. I find a soft, plastic eraser the most satisfactory for general purposes and a putty rubber useful for lifting charcoal and carbon passages to produce highlights.

Conté

Fine nib

No 6 brush

Charcoal

Four sketches in different media

5

Hatching

Cross hatching

Shaded foliage

Curved hatching

Grass

Using pen and ink

Line drawing with Indian ink has long been a popular method of illustration, much appreciated by printers, for the crisp, black lines are relatively easy to reproduce. It is a versatile technique, in that it can cope with a wide variety of tones and textures and is capable of rendering the smallest detail. It is particularly useful for small drawings, but rather less so for the larger variety. I prefer to use a flexible nib, capable of producing both fine and thick lines. Fine lines are used for drawing and shading distant objects, as they produce a greyish effect which suggests recession. Foreground objects are treated more boldly with strong, black lines which bring them forward. Smooth papers are normally used so that the pen can glide over the surface without snagging.

Tone is achieved by 'hatching', which consists of drawing a series of regularly spaced parallel lines to produce an overall impression of grey. The closer the lines, and the less the white space between them, the deeper will be the tone of the resulting grey. A second series of lines can be drawn, at an angle to the first, to deepen and vary the shading and this is termed 'cross hatching'. Lines of shading need not necessarily be straight and may equally well be curved, to help describe a curvilinear surface. Hatching may be used in conjunction with broken and discontinuous marks to describe, for example, shadowed foliage, and most artists develop many variations of their own.

Sketch 1 relies for its impact on counterchange, the light tones of the sunlit bridge contrasting with the dark undersides of the arches and the shadowed gables beyond. The vertical forms of the oast houses and tall trees provide a foil for the predominantly horizontal lines of the bridge and the water. The reflections in the river are indicated by a series of horizontal strokes which help to establish the flat surface of the water and also suggest some slight movement, due to the river current.

The old mill house in Sketch 2 is largely surrounded by foliage, the treatment of which has been varied to provide tonal contrast. Where the buildings are in shade, the foliage is comparatively light; where they are in sunlight, the tone of the foliage is much deeper. The small willow tree on the right is set against the darker trees beyond, again to obtain tonal contrast. The footpath carries the eye into the centre of the drawing and the old man is also moving into the scene, albeit slowly! The reflections in the water are built up with a series of vertical marks, to suggest still water.

Pen and ink can sometimes prove a rather hard and uncompromising medium for capturing the soft gradations of nature, but used in conjuction with black Conté pencil this problem can be overcome. The broken marks made by the Conté blend well with the black lines of the Indian ink and introduce a welcome softness. I used this technique in Sketch 3, of the bend in the river Ouse above Lewes. A rough paper would be too coarse for this treatment but a watercolour Not has just the right amount of tooth.

Sketch 1: river bridge

Sketch 2: water mill

Sketch 3: bend in the river

Using felt-tip pens

Markers and felt-tip pens are comparative newcomers to the art scene. Their colours are somewhat harsh and uncompromising for normal landscape work but the blacks and greys can be useful drawing implements. The tips come in a variety of sizes; fine, medium and thick. Some of the heavy varieties have oblique, chisel-shaped ends which enable the user to produce lines of varying thickness. They vary in other ways too; some are water-soluble, others permanent; some are fade-resistant, others much less so. The ink registers strongly and quickly sinks into the surface of the paper. On the softer and more absorbent varieties of paper it tends to spread, to produce unintentionally heavy marks. On the credit side, these pens are inexpensive and can produce quick and spontaneous effects, so they are well worth some experiment, provided their limitations are borne in mind. Always buy the fade-resistant variety and make sure you know whether your purchases are water-soluble or not.

Try them out on off cuts of different types of paper to discover which is most suitable for your purpose and then experiment with them until you become familiar with the way they behave. You will find that if you use them slowly and deliberately, they will deposit a lot of ink on the paper and make very black and solid marks; if you wield them with greater speed and panache, so

Devon estuary

Downs with foreground tree and figure

that they skate over the surface of the paper, you will obtain lighter and more broken effects and these will bring variety and expressiveness to your work.

Because they tend to produce lines of uniform thickness, it is a good plan to use pens with tips of varying sizes in your drawings. The fine tips can be used for distant objects, as their lighter lines will suggest recession, and the thicker reserved for the stronger treatment of the foreground. Another way of achieving a feeling of recession is to use a grey pen rather than a black for more distant objects, as I have done in these sketches. The lighter, softer tone has a greying effect which pushes distant objects into the background. If you adopt this plan, do not reserve the grey pen only for the distance but introduce it, where it can serve a useful purpose, into other passages as well. This will help to hold your drawing together and prevent it appearing as two distinct and unrelated halves.

For my taste, the inherent lack of subtlety of felt-tip pens makes them more suitable for lightning sketches than for finished drawings, and they can be extremely useful for recording quick impressions. The sketch, on grey tinted paper, of the Devon estuary, was literally made in five minutes, though I added the white chalk later to provide a little tonal contrast. The second sketch, also in black and grey felt-tip, took no longer, though I added the figure and the dog afterwards to give balance and interest. Both sketches could serve as a basis for later, more elaborate drawings.

Perspective

Many people experience great difficulty with perspective and often allow faults to persist in their work long after they have left other elementary mistakes behind them. This is unfortunate, for mastering the rules of perspective is not a difficult matter and once this has been achieved, the problems disappear. A knowledge of perspective is not so vital in drawing such objects as trees and fields, but buildings, bridges and roads occur in landscape subjects and here an understanding is essential. Even cloudy skies are subject to the laws of perspective and we need to know enough to avoid drawing rivers that appear to flow uphill!

Perspective is based upon the observable fact that objects appear smaller the farther away they are and that beyond a certain point they disappear altogether. This is shown diagramatically in Fig 1, in which the line of telegraph poles seems to disappear at the point on the flat horizon, known as the 'vanishing point'.

In Fig 2, there are two vanishing points on the true horizon, or at eye level. Notice that we are not concerned with the observable horizon which may well be modified by rising ground. Only in the case of the sea, or a dead level plain, will the true and the observable horizons coincide.

Fig 3 demonstrates how much steeper the perspective lines are when the object in question is close at hand and how much flatter they are when it is farther away. In Fig 4 we see how objects that are not parallel have different vanishing points.

The perspective of reflections often causes difficulty; the trick here is to imagine the flat plane of the water surface continuing right to the foot of the object reflected, and the construction in Fig 5 indicates how much of the reflection we will see. Finally, the construction in Fig 6 tells us how to determine the size and position of cast shadows.

With practice, perspective becomes intuitive but until that happy day these constructions will enable you to check your drawings against gross error.

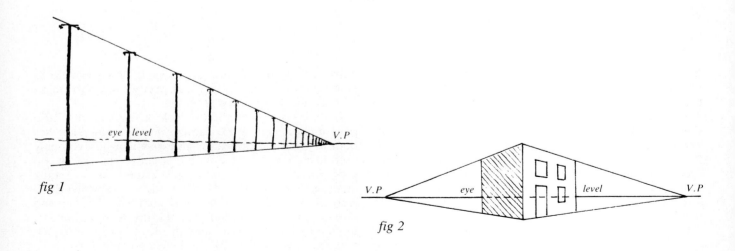

fig 1

fig 2

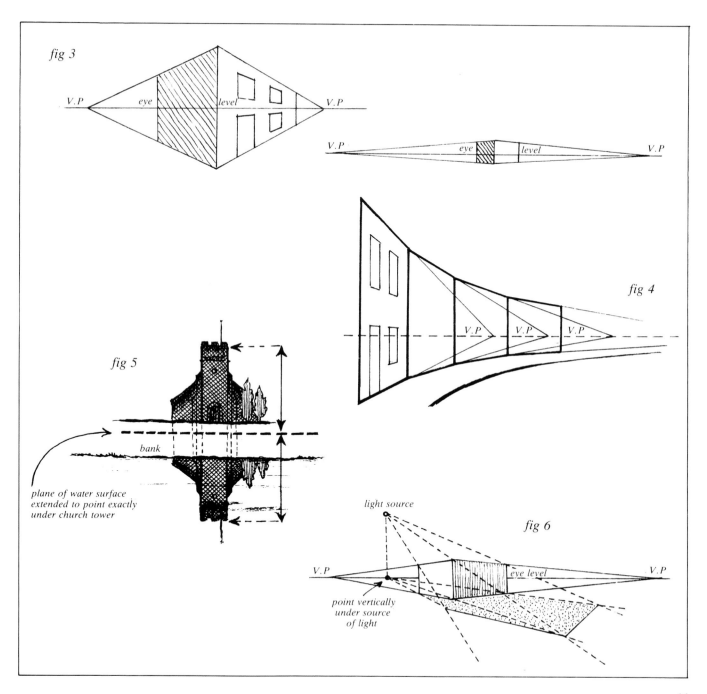

fig 3

V.P   *eye*   *level*   V.P

V.P   *eye*   *level*   V.P

fig 4

V.P   V.P   V.P

fig 5

bank

*plane of water surface
extended to point exactly
under church tower*

light source

fig 6

V.P   *eye level*   V.P

*point vertically
under source
of light*

11

Composition

The concept of good composition is a somewhat vague one and it is easier to recognise a well composed drawing than it is to rationalise its success. Suffice to say that a drawing that has good composition is one in which the subject matter is so arranged that the overall effect is pleasing and satisfying.

Artists came to believe that their rectangular canvasses could be divided up horizontally and vertically in an ideal manner and that if the main elements of the drawing fell on these divisions, perfect proportion would result. This theory was formalised in the invention of the 'golden mean', or 'divine proportion', as it was sometimes termed.

To divide a line of any length into this ideal proportion a geometric construction is necessary, (see Fig 1). The line A to B is extended by half its length to C and a vertical line A to D, equal in length to A to B, is drawn from point A. With the point of a compass on C as the centre, and C to D as the radius, describe an arc to cut A to B at point E. Point E now divides the line A to B in the ideal proportion. By producing line A to B to the right instead of the left, and using the same method, a second point, E1, will be found which also divides the line in the ideal proportion.

Fig 2 shows a rectangle ABCD in which all four sides have been divided up in this way and the resulting points are marked, E, E1, E2 up to E7. The lines joining the opposite points E indicate the golden means of the rectangle. The artist will try to place the salient features of his painting on these lines, to achieve compositional harmony.

If all this seems Greek to you, and if the standard of your geometry is not up to that of your art, you may find it easier to recognize the most common faults in composition without reference to Euclid. Here, then, are some of the pitfalls to avoid:−

1) Avoid placing a dominant horizontal or vertical line right in the middle of your paper, dividing it into exactly equal halves.

2) Avoid placing a dominant line, such as the edge of a road, in such a manner that it originates in one corner of your paper.

3) Avoid placing all the tonal weight on one side of your paper.

4) Avoid making unrelated lines coincide. For example, do not let the ridge of a roof exactly coincide with a line of distant hills.

5) Avoid including, uncritically, every object, however inharmonious, in the view before you. A long line of regular fencing, for example, is best omitted, or at least modified.

6) Avoid drawing figures, vehicles, boats, etc., which are moving out of the drawing, for they carry the eye out of the picture instead of into it.

Shady lane

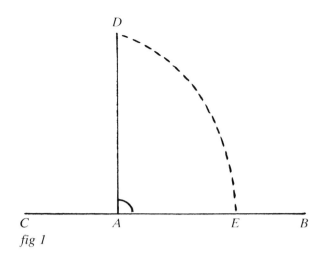

fig 1

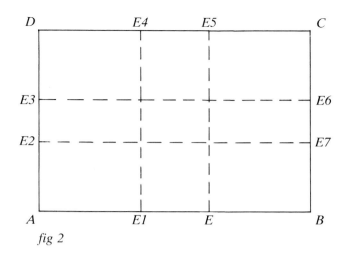

fig 2

These faults all occur in the rather unattractive Fig 3 and are corrected in Fig 4 in which, incidentally, the church spire is placed on the 'golden mean'! Another common fault, which I could not squeeze into Fig 3, is that of having two focal points instead of one – a forking road leading the eye to two competing centres of interest would be an example of this.

With increasing experience pleasing composition will in time become second nature. It is always good practice to make several quick sketches of your chosen subject, from varying viewpoints, before finally deciding upon your composition. This will exercise your critical faculties and increase your awareness of the dictates of sound composition.

fig 3

fig 4

13

Choosing and developing subjects

A student on one of my courses once spent several hours looking for a subject to draw, despite the fact that we were in a delightful farming area, with a wealth of material from which to choose. The problem was that she had a preconceived and rigid idea of what she wanted to draw, and so her mind was closed to everything else.

The artist should cultivate an open mind, receptive at all times to external impressions and stimuli. With such an attitude we do not have to look very far, for subjects will quickly present themselves and evoke a response. The chosen subject need not be a conventionally attractive landscape and could equally well be a group of humble farm implements by a barn door, or any one of a thousand other possibilities. The important thing is that something about the subject should strike a chord and challenge us to say something fresh and exciting about it. Only thus will we be able to convey to others something more than a mere pictorial likeness.

One of the problems that causes inexperienced artists constant difficulty is that of separating a promising subject from a mass of surrounding, irrelevant detail. A grand panorama that would daunt a Constable seems to have an irresistible appeal, when a small section of it would make a far more satisfactory subject. This is where a home-made viewfinder is so helpful; this is simply a rectangle of stiff card with an aperture about the size of a postcard cut in it. By holding it up to an extensive vista, one can readily isolate more manageable sections of it. The area within the aperture can be increased or diminished by moving the viewfinder towards or away from the eye.

All sorts of considerations enter into our choice of subject. Pleasing composition comes high on the list and interplay of light and shade runs it a close second. Are there good areas of light to be set against strong dark areas to provide effective and sometimes dramatic contrast?

Most landscape subjects can be tackled from a number of different viewpoints and, as we noted earlier, it is a good plan to make several quick sketches from various vantage points. This will help you explore the subject in depth and a comparison of the sketches will probably help you decide which yields the most pleasing composition. The two small sketches, (opposite), are quick Conté impressions of a simple landscape subject from different viewpoints and the one that appealed to me formed the basis of the finished larger drawing.

Try to keep your sketches and drawings free and loose. There is nothing more inhibiting than a tight, exact style with not a line out of place. Your first, exploratory strokes should be light and tentative, never hard and uncompromising. As your drawing develops, those that are significant can be strengthened and the remainder ignored.

Farm gate

Preliminary sketches

Finished drawing

15

Buildings in the landscape

However remote the terrain, there is usually evidence of human habitation to be seen and buildings of some sort are more often than not an integral part of the landscape. Older buildings have a way of settling into the countryside, constructed as they normally are of local materials. The rugged stone cottages of Cornwall, for example, appear almost to be extensions of the granite outcrops of that area.

Well placed buildings can add point to a landscape and act as centres of interest. Church towers and spires, with their strong vertical lines, have a particular part to play in this context, as Constable demonstrated in 'The Cornfield'. The geometric shapes of buildings provide a useful contrast to the softer and more rounded forms of nature and there is contrast, too, in texture and tone.

Some landscape subjects are, of course, almost entirely man-made and need be no less attractive for that. The accompanying sketch, drawn with a steel nib in Indian ink, shows a Cotswold lane and a group of old stone cottages with a few bare trees in the background. The gazebo and the foreground walls were close enough to require the drawing of individual stones; the odd random stone in the more distant cottages merely suggests the building material. Notice that the old gentleman is walking into the drawing, and not out of it!

Cotswold lane

Sketching in the field

Having chosen our drawing materials, studied such topics as perspective and composition and considered the important matter of selecting and developing subjects, we are now in a position to sally forth into the countryside and sketch to our heart's content. What could be more pleasurable than the promise of fine weather and the prospect of a day's uninterrupted sketching? At this stage we shall concentrate on identifying as many promising subjects as we can and sketching them quickly and boldly, perhaps from several different viewpoints. This approach will not only develop our artistic awareness of our surroundings but will improve our sketching technique. It will also provide a host of ideas and images, some of which will later form the basis for full-sized drawings.

We will avoid towns and main roads and explore leafy lanes, byways and farm tracks. Whenever a promising subject presents itself, we will stop and make a quick sketch, bearing in mind that we are not looking for the grand panorama but for glimpses of the countryside which will make simple but attractive compositions. You will find that such unpretentious subjects will provide you with a wealth of promising and exciting material.

Opposite are a few sketches of the countryside near my home, all made one fine autumn day. I used a 4B pencil on Not watercolour paper in pad form and concentrated on capturing the essence of the scene and eliminating all unnecessary detail. As I was not making accurate drawings of particular places, I felt free to vary the positions of some of the elements in the scenes I was sketching, to improve the composition.

Sketch 1 consists of a country lane, a few trees and a line of distant hills. Notice how the lane winds back into the middle distance and does not carry the eye out of the drawing. Notice, too, how the shadows of the trees on the right fall across the lane and help to describe the contours of the surface on which they fall. The clouds on the left help to provide tonal balance and as the sky was an interesting one, I adopted a low horizon, to do it justice. The small figure provides scale and acts as a focal point.

In sketch 2, I was more interested in the land than the sky, so I decided upon a high horizon, about two-thirds of the way up the paper. The little stone bridge provides the centre of interest and its light tone helps it to stand out against the dark bank of trees beyond. Notice how the lines of the river banks lead the eye towards this bridge and how the nearer trees on the right, together with their reflections, help to balance the dark tones on the left of the drawing.

Sketch 3 includes a small group of farm buildings and, once again, the lane carries the eye into the heart of the drawing. The sunlit roofs stand out against the darker trees behind and the nearer tree on the right helps to provide tonal balance. The deep shadow of a tree just out of the sketch to the right provides some interest and tonal contrast in what would otherwise have been a rather flat and uninteresting foreground.

Sketch 4 features the estuary of a small river with an impression of the medieval town of Rye, perched on its little hill, forming the background. With the exception of this hill, the terrain is flat and the low horizon helps to emphasize this quality. The lines of the river banks do not emanate from the corners of the paper and the river is prevented from carrying the eye off the paper by the group of bushes on the left, which acts as a buffer. The moored boats help to balance the dark silhouette of the little town and the subdued tones of the banks contrast with the pale tone of the water and make it shine.

Sketch 1

Sketch 2

Sketch 3

Sketch 4

19

Drawing trees

Trees form a vital part of the landscape and so require particularly careful study. I included a number of trees in the sketches which illustrated the previous section, but they were the merest impressions, not drawn in any detail. We shall now consider form and structure in greater depth.

Many students experience great difficulty in drawing trees and often get bogged down in a hopeless attempt to draw every leaf and twig. When one considers the number of leaves on the average tree, it is obvious that this approach is doomed to failure. It is far better to look at trees through half-closed eyes, thus eliminating the finer detail, for the broad areas of light and shade that then become apparent respond far more readily to the pencil.

One of the commonest faults in landscape drawing is the failure to distinguish between the tone of trees and that of fields. Fields are flat and reflect the maximum amount of light from the sky above, whereas trees are vertical forms and not only is that half of the tree away from the sun in shade, but many of the lower branches are shadowed by those above. Moreover, trees are often seen against a luminous sky and this makes them appear even darker than they are. When one adds to all this the observable fact that the leaves of most trees are a darker colour than blades of grass, one can understand the reason for this obvious difference in tone.

Another common fault, which stems, like most faults, from lack of careful observation, is that of making the limbs and branches too sinuous and snake-like and ignoring their angularity. Branches facing the artist are more difficult to draw than those that stretch out to the left and right and are often omitted altogether by beginners! The manner in which branches are attached to the trunk is another area in which evidence of close observation is often painfully lacking. Sketch 1 shows the symmetry of bare trees.

In sketch 2 the tree is considerably darker in tone than the greensward below. It also boasts branches growing in all directions, not just to the left and right!

Careful observation of the effects of light and shade shows us the manner in which the shadows of foliage and branches, falling across the main trunk, are modified by its cylindrical form. Sketch 3 illustrates this point. Tree shadows are often drawn by beginners as though falling across a billiard table surface instead of being modified by the irregularity of that surface. We noted earlier how tree shadows, lying across a lane, can help to describe the surface form of that lane, its camber and its banks. Tree shadows can play another important role in breaking up the over-insistent lines of a road or track.

One sometimes comes across stands of trees which form particularly pleasing groups. These are always worth recording, not least, perhaps, for incorporating into some future drawing. Sketches 4 and 5, are examples from my own sketchbook.

Sketch 1: bare trees

Sketch 2: single tree

Sketch 3:
section of trunk

Sketch 4: group of conifers

Sketch 5: dead tree by a river

Water in the landscape

Rivers, streams, lakes, and ponds occur very frequently in the landscape and, indeed, contribute greatly to its variety and beauty. They are of particular interest to the artist, for they provide him with that which he is constantly seeking – contrast. Contrast of form occurs when a flat sheet of water acts as a foil to the vertical shapes of the fringing trees; contrast of tone results from the counterchange between a shining expanse of water and the darker terrain beside it. Water gives the landscape artist an extra dimension in his work and we shall now consider how best to incorporate it into our drawing and do it the justice it merits.

Rivers and streams, correctly observed, can carry the eye deep into the heart of the drawing and this is an extra bonus. They should never be allowed to carry the eye straight off the paper. In the pencil sketch, below, the shining water of the river disappears round a bend and is not permitted to continue, uninterrupted, to the edge of the drawing. The perspective has been carefully handled so that the water lies flat and does not appear to be flowing uphill, as is sometimes the case with the work of beginners! When a local breeze ruffles the surface of the water, the sky above is reflected rather than the landscape beyond and this gives rise to a stretch of pale toned water. This can sometimes be put to useful effect by separating the scene beyond the water from its reflection. This device has been used in the river sketch, below, and in the drawing of the lake opposite.

Very calm, unruffled water acts as a mirror and so produces a mirror image of the scene above. This can look attractive in photographs but is best avoided by the artist in the majority of cases. Unless the scene is a particularly simple and uncluttered one, an inverted replica below usually leads to over-elaboration and confusion. Except on abnormally still days, there is usually a slight ruffling of the water's surface and this causes a softening and a diffusion of the reflection. In this way the reflection complements the scene above instead of competing with it.

Mountain lake

Pencil sketch of river

Figures in the landscape

Some landscape subjects rely for their impact upon a brooding sense of solitude and loneliness and in these the presence of human figures would be intrusive. In other cases, well placed figures can act as focal points and add life and interest to a scene. They can also serve to lend scale to drawings and tiny figures can add greatly to the impact of, for example, mountain scenery.

In town and village drawings, figures are, of course, necessary to give realism to scenes which are normally peopled. Their treatment should be in harmony with that of their setting and background. They should not be given special prominence or sharper delineation, or they will cease to be an integral part of the scene. At the same time they should not appear static or wooden. As with so much in art, practice is the answer, and a sketch book, filled with quick impressions of the human figure, will be of immense value when convincing examples are required for particular purposes.

In the lake-side scene below, I used black and white Conté and grey chalk on a pale grey ground. The scene

Anglers by a lake

Figures in a lane

would have been somewhat empty without the figures, which add interest and provide a focal point. Notice how they are placed against a pale patch of water, to provide tonal contrast. The more distant trees on the left and their reflections provide compositional balance.

The sketch of the tree-lined lane, above, was made in Indian ink. The bold treatment emphasizes the strong verticals of the trees and their equally strong lateral shadows. The line of these shadows helps to describe the contours of the surface on which they fall, in the manner described in the section on 'Sketching in the field' on page 18. The small figures, moving into the picture, supply scale and emphasize the height of the bare trees on the left.

25

Drawing coastal scenery

The margin between land and sea has always held a particular fascination for the artist and there is no doubt that it provides an endless supply of appealing subjects. Not only has the sea fashioned a wide range of natural cliff formations, which can vary enormously according to the composition and hardness of the coastal rock, but man has made his own contribution, sometimes harmoniously, sometimes, alas, the reverse.

The older fishing villages, built of local stone, are a rich source of material and their solid masonry and their quaint, unplanned outlines invite our attention. The sea itself, in all its moods, presents the artist with a unique challenge to which he can only hope to respond successfully after much painstaking study. Huge waves crashing on the shore, gentle ripples reflecting boats and buildings in sheltered havens and the many variations between these two extremes, all consist of moving water which he has to freeze mentally at a moment in time, and capture without losing the essential feeling of movement.

Sketch 1

Coastal scenery, of course, also includes the shoreline, and we are equally concerned with sandy beaches, craggy rocks, cliffs, harbours, buildings, boats of all types and, of course, the salty characters who inhabit such places! All demand close and careful observation and practice. Boats seem to cause particular difficulty and many a marine drawing has been spoilt by some ill-drawn craft of unseaworthy appearance. The subtle lines of keel and gunwale present problems but richly repay study. So take your sketchbook down to the nearest harbour and spend a glorious day drawing anything and everything you see. Your skill will develop and you will quickly accumulate a stock of fascinating material for possible future use.

Sketch 1 is a quick, thumbnail impression of a harbour scene, made in a few seconds with a 4B pencil and is one of several made while I was experimenting with a number of different viewpoints. Sketch 2, drawn in Indian ink, is a rather more complex arrangement of boats moored in a sheltered

Sketch 2

estuary, with washes of diluted ink added to provide tone. Sketches 3 and 4 were both made with sticks of charcoal on Not watercolour paper. In both cases the charcoal was rubbed to provide smooth passages for sky and sea but the texture of the paper was utilised to depict the rough grass and scrub of the foregrounds.

In sketch 3 white paper represents chalk cliffs in full light and a putty rubber was used to suggest their reflections in the smooth sea. Tonal contrast has been exploited wherever possible – the distant cliff-top grass against the luminous sky, the white cliffs against the darker water below, and so on. The rough track leads the eye into the centre of interest of the drawing and the dark cliff-top on the left balances the deep tones on the right of the composition.

Sketch 4, a quick impression of a track leading down to the beach, contains little detail, but the lively clouds are full of movement and, with the windswept trees, suggest squally weather. Charcoal is an expressive medium which readily conveys atmosphere.

Sketch 4

Industrial landscapes

In the minds of many people the word 'landscape' is virtually synonymous with 'countryside' and it would not occur to them that built-up and industrial areas have just as much claim to that title. I would be the last to criticise those who draw their inspiration from predominantly rural subjects, for they are recording something that is both precious and vulnerable. But artists should be concerned with the total environment, not just one attractive aspect of it, and they should learn to respond to the rich and often dramatic possibilities that industry frequently has to offer. I have heard people say that they are not interested in drawing ugliness for its own sake and that there is already quite enough squalor in the world without adding to it. This attitude, though understandable, misinterprets the nature of art. Drawings are, after all, just a series of related marks, and whatever their source of inspiration, they can be harmonious, well composed and pleasing.

Industrial subjects can be strongly atmospheric and can fire the receptive imagination. On the debit side, they frequently contain a bewildering amount of detail, but if one concentrates on conveying atmosphere and feeling, and greatly simplifies the detail, the rewards can be great. One way of simplifying the subject matter is to select drawing implements that will not allow you to add fiddly detail. There are several that fill the bill, including charcoal and marker pens.

The first sketch, below, is of a river running through

Industrial river

Mining valley

an area of heavy industry. For this I used thick black and grey marker pens, boldly and directly. The distance was put in with the grey to form a pale silhouette, while for the nearer features I used black for the shadowed areas, leaving the white paper to represent those catching the light. I used the grey marker pen here and there to tone down some of the white areas and so unify, to some extent, foreground and background. I used a fine felt-tip pen to add just a little detail but did not attempt to tidy up the rough lines made by the thick, black marker pen. Finally, I put in the cloudy sky with charcoal, which I then rubbed gently with a cloth to obtain the soft effect I wanted. Just a quick impression, but with something to say about its subject.

The mining village, above, was sketched in charcoal and the finer detail put in with a well sharpened Conté. I did a little gentle rubbing of the charcoal to soften the sky and the far hillside, but the boldness of the charcoal and the roughness of the paper surface combined to suggest the ruggedness of the foreground. The stream and the footpath both lead the eye into the drawing. The dark mass of rocky hillside on the left serves to balance the miners' cottages on the right and tonal contrast has been emphasized wherever possible. This quick and bold style of drawing relies heavily for its success upon counterchange – the placing of lights against darks and darks against lights. It is fun to do, so why not try it for yourself?

29

Drawing in the snow

The appearance of the landscape is deeply affected by the changing seasons but never more so than when the fields and trees are mantled with snow. The tonal balance of the countryside is inverted, for now the land surface is much lighter than the sky and if the clouds are still heavy with snow, this reversal of normal tone values can be dramatic. As artists, we are tempted to emphasize and even exaggerate this effect for it is a sure way of highlighting the whiteness of the snow. By the same token, the snow will appear to darken the tone of everything that stands upon it – trees, hedges, buildings, telegraph poles and so on. I say 'appear to darken' advisedly, because in absolute terms the light reflecting from the snow can only heighten the tone of these objects but the eye tells us they are darker, and we must draw what we see.

Heavy snowfalls affect form as well as tone and iron out the irregularities of the land under a smooth sweep of white. They also soften and round out the sharp angles of roofs and other man-made objects on which they fall.

We have to admit that painters have the edge when it comes to capturing the effects of the wintry scene, for they can do justice to the subtle blues and greens of shadows falling across the snow and the even more subtle warm hues when the sun is low. However, by the careful and imaginative use of tonal contrast, we can create effective snowscapes of our own and capture something of the atmosphere of the winter landscape.

Sketch 1, of oast houses and barns, was drawn with pen and ink, with just a little pale wash to darken the sky and describe the shadows. It relies for its effect upon the contrast between the shining snow and the dark tones of the farm buildings, trees and hedges.

For sketch 2, I used a scraperboard, a black-coated card on which one draws with small blades of various shapes mounted in a penholder. The black coating is scraped away to reveal the white underneath and in this way the drawing is gradually built up. Scraperboard drawings sometimes have the appearance of woodcuts when printed and are often confused with the older medium.

Sketch 3, of a snowy landscape, was made with a graphite pencil, a pleasant, fluent drawing implement. The strong hatching of the sky imparts a whiteness to the snow, as does the comparatively heavy treatment of the trees and hedges. The large tree on the left balances the tree-fringed hamlet on the right. The foreground road, with its line of telegraph poles, could easily carry the eye off the right-hand margin of the paper, but the church is such an obvious focal point that the eye automatically turns left at the T-junction and no harm is done.

Sketch 1

Sketch 2

Sketch 3

First Published in Great Britain 1990
Search Press Ltd,
Wellwood, North Farm Road,
Tunbridge Wells, Kent TN2 3DR

Text and drawings by Ray Campbell Smith

U.S. Artists Materials Trade Distributors:
Winsor & Newton, Inc.
11 Constitution Avenue, P.O. Box 1396, Piscataway, NJ
08855-1396

Canadian Distributors:
Anthes Universal Limited
341 Heart Lake Road South, Brampton, Ontario L6W 3K8

Australian Distributors:
Jasco Pty Limited
937-941 Victoria Road, West Ryde, N.S.W. 2114

New Zealand Distributors:
Caldwell Wholesale Limited
Wellington and Auckland

ISBN 0 85532 641 7

The Nile

Phototypeset by Scribe Design, 123 Watling Street,
Gillingham, Kent
Made and printed in Spain by A.G. Elkar S. Coop. Bilbao-12